MODERN ROLE MODELS

Chris Rock

David Robson

Mason Crest Publishers

D1466206

Produced by OTTN Publishing in association with
21st Century Publishing and Communications, Inc.

Copyright © 2009 by Mason Crest Publishers. All rights reserved. No part of this
publication may be reproduced or transmitted in any form or by any means,
electronic or mechanical, including photocopying, recording, taping, or any
information storage and retrieval system, without permission from the publisher.

MASON CREST PUBLISHERS INC.
370 Reed Road
Broomall, Pennsylvania 19008
(866) MCP-BOOK (toll free)
www.masoncrest.com

Printed in the United States of America.

First Printing

9 8 7 6 5 4 3 2 1

Library of Congress Cataloging-in-Publication Data

Robson, David, 1966–
   Chris Rock / David Robson.
     p. cm.— (Modern role models)
   ISBN 978-1-4222-0506-8 (hardcover) — ISBN 978-1-4222-0793-2 (pbk.)
   1. Rock, Chris—Juvenile literature. 2. Comedians—United States—Biography—
Juvenile literature. 3. Actors—United States—Biography—Juvenile literature.
I. Title.
PN2287.R717R63 2008
792.702'8092—dc22
[B]   2008025302

Publisher's note:
All quotations in this book come from original sources, and contain the spelling
and grammatical inconsistencies of the original text.

CROSS-CURRENTS

In the ebb and flow of the currents of life we are each influenced
by many people, places, and events that we directly experience
or have learned about. Throughout the chapters of this book you
will come across **CROSS-CURRENTS** reference boxes. These
boxes direct you to a **CROSS-CURRENTS** section in the back
of the book that contains fascinating and informative sidebars
and related pictures. Go on. ▸▸

CONTENTS

Chris Rock brought his take-no-prisoners comedy to the 77th Annual Academy Awards on February 27, 2005 in Los Angeles, California. The Hollywood stars and millions of viewers who watched Chris host the ceremony had mixed responses. Some found his jokes tasteless, while others were amused. But Chris's humor has always been controversial, forcing people to pay attention.

1

The Big Time

COMEDIAN CHRIS ROCK HAS NEVER PLAYED IT safe. From his early days playing stand-up **gigs** in New York City comedy clubs to his work in popular films such as *Madagascar*, Rock became known for his honesty and attitude and, sometimes, for offending people along the way. The world according to Chris Rock is a surprising and very funny place.

Years of hard work, including jobs on the ever-popular network comedy program *Saturday Night Live* and his own Emmy Award–winning late night talk show on HBO, *The Chris Rock Show*, have earned Chris a level of fame that many entertainers can only dream of achieving. Chris's comedy is controversial. He speaks about race, politics, and marriage in sharp, curse-filled rants. His comments can be brutal, yet his fans see that there is much honesty in what he says. More than once he has been called the funniest man in the world. By 2005 Chris Rock was also one of the highest paid and most popular funnymen of his generation.

It was, therefore, no surprise when Gil Cates, producer of the 77th annual **Academy Awards**, asked Chris to host the awards ceremony in early 2005. Widely seen as the most important event in the entertainment industry, the show, also known as the Oscars, is watched by more than a billion people around the world every year. Movie stars walk the red carpet, hand out golden trophies for excellence in filmmaking, and afterward hold grand parties in honor of themselves. For several years Billy Crystal, a popular comedian, had hosted the Academy Awards ceremonies. Crystal had always received warm praise for his work on the show, but he was busy with another project and couldn't do the program in 2005. So Cates decided to take a risk and try to win more viewers with a younger, hipper host.

CROSS-CURRENTS

Read "Oscar Hosting: A Prime Gig" to find out more about the benefits of hosting the annual Academy Awards ceremony. Go to page 46. ▶▶

Chris was not an entirely unexpected choice—Cates had asked him to host the show as far back as 1997. And Chris had some experience as an awards-show host, having performed that role at MTV's Video Music Awards in 1997, 1999, and 2003. He had also presented awards at the Oscars in the past.

⇒ DANGER AHEAD ⇐

The hiring of Chris Rock as host of the Academy Awards ceremony sent a clear message to viewers that unpredictability would be the theme of that year's show. Chris was just the man for the job, or so it seemed. In an interview with *Entertainment Weekly* magazine that was published shortly before the big event, Chris caused a stir. First, he commented that many black people—particularly black men— did not watch the Oscars. As if that was not controversial enough, when asked whether he planned on toning down his outspoken humor, Rock said he did, but just barely:

> **“I agree not to curse and then I stay out of people's way. . . . I'm a fastball pitcher, so I'm gonna be throwing fastballs. No time to fool around with what works now. . . . You gotta do what you do.”**

And throw fastballs he did. When Chris walked across the stage as host of the Academy Awards on February 27, 2005, he was greeted

By the time Chris was invited to host the 2005 Academy Awards, he was being called the funniest man in America. Chris has said that he is surprised to receive such high praise. There are so many different ways to make people laugh, he says, that it is impossible to determine which is the funniest.

with a standing ovation from the audience. But then the somewhat old-fashioned Oscar audience became the butt of Chris's jokes, as he poked fun at self-centered and **arrogant** movie stars. He made a point of showing Hollywood how out-of-touch it was with everyday people. In one previously taped piece, Chris interviewed black men and women. He asked them if they had heard of or seen any of the Oscar-nominated films, which included director Martin Scorsese's *The Aviator* and Clint Eastwood's *Million Dollar Baby*. They had not. In his opening speech, he made fun of current movie stars, such

CHRIS ROCK

Chris's skits and monologues at the 2005 Academy Awards were as fearless as his stand-up shows. Still, Chris has said that he pulls certain punches during awards ceremonies. For example, when he jokes about public figures, he tries to focus on their careers instead of making fun of their personal lives. He also avoids mocking teenage celebrities.

as Jude Law, hinting that they were far less talented than legendary actors of the past, such as Cary Grant.

Chris's take-no-prisoners approach left some in the audience at the Kodak Theatre sitting in stunned silence. After the show, several critics, such as award-winning entertainment writer Tom Shales, put down Chris's work, calling it mean and unfunny. Looking back today, Chris disagrees with that assessment:

> **“They always write that it went badly, but show me the jokes that didn't work. The house was actually pulling for me. . . . So much weird concern.”**

➤ OSCARS AND BEYOND ◀

In spite of the mixed reaction to his Oscar gig, Chris has hardly slowed down. By Oscar night he had already won two Emmys for his HBO series, *The Chris Rock Show*. He was also working on a new project: a comedy series based on his childhood years growing up in Brooklyn, New York. The show, *Everybody Hates Chris*, began airing on the UPN network in the fall of 2005. *Everybody Hates Chris* quickly became one of the network's biggest hits.

CROSS-CURRENTS

To learn more about the life and career of a ground-breaking African-American comedian, read "Richard Pryor: Comedy Legend." Go to page 46. ▶▶

Meanwhile, Chris wrote and directed two feature films and continues to take his comedy act on the road, most recently with his *No Apologies* tour. For the first time, Chris has even gone overseas—to London, New Zealand, and South Africa. His comic empire continues to grow, as does his family. Chris devotes time and effort to **charitable** causes, including the Salvation Army and programs that teach people to read. For a comedian whose career resulted more from accident than from careful planning, Chris Rock's place near the peak of the comedy mountain demonstrates that talent, intelligence, and hard work will rise to the top eventually.

Chris Rock grew up in a lower-income area in Brooklyn, New York, developing his comic timing at an early age to cope with racist bullies at school. Before breaking into television and movies, Chris performed in New York City's comedy clubs. On much larger stages, he still demonstrates the same sharp wit he developed before becoming famous.

2

The Brooklyn Boy Gets His Shot

CHRISTOPHER JULIUS ROCK III WAS BORN TO A middle-class family in Andrews, South Carolina, on February 7, 1965. His father, Julius, worked as a truck driver. Rose, his mother, taught school. Chris remembers little of his time in the South; the family moved to Brooklyn, New York, when he was just a few years old.

Chris was the eldest of seven children in the family: Tony, Brian, Andre, Kenny, Andi, and a half-brother, Jordon. In school Chris was a class clown, a jokester. Yet the schools he went to had mostly white students, and Chris was sometimes taunted and made fun of because he was black. He escaped such painful experiences by trying to be funny.

While in high school, he began hanging out at comedy clubs in the New York City area, including the legendary Catch a Rising Star. Chris performed during open-mike nights—slow nights at the clubs during which anyone with a comedy routine could take the stage and give performing his or her best shot. The work gave Chris a sense of accomplishment and belonging he had never known before. Night after night his confidence grew. He saw what worked and what didn't. As Chris Rock later said, he began to understand what made people laugh:

> **"I figure that laughter sometimes starts from pain. You might wince, but then I know that I'm doing my job. The only thing I can do wrong is not be funny."**

Finding some success as a young comedian also convinced Chris to drop out of high school before graduation. It was a risk he was willing to take. He was betting that he could make a career of his comedy routine. All he needed was a break.

⟫ COMIC FATE ⟪

In 1987 superstar comedian and actor Eddie Murphy was in New York City. Since the early 1980s—first on NBC's *Saturday Night Live* and then in a string of hit movies, such as *Trading Places*, *48 Hours*, and *Beverly Hills Cop*—Murphy had been gaining fame and breaking box-office records. His **profane** but popular brand of humor earned him millions of dollars and placed him high atop the list of the biggest movie stars in the world.

Murphy was always on the lookout for fresh-faced newcomers, and one evening he popped into a local comedy club. A young comedian, Chris Rock, was scheduled to perform. Unpolished though he was, Chris was clever, insightful, and laugh-out-loud funny.

CROSS-CURRENTS

If you would like to learn more about Eddie Murphy's life and career, check out "The '80s King of Comedy." Go to page 48. ▶▶

After Chris's set, Murphy approached him, struck up a conversation, and offered Chris a small part in his upcoming movie, *Beverly Hills Cop II*. Following his work in Murphy's film, Chris landed small but memorable parts in a string of movies, most notably the well-received **blaxploitation** spoof *I'm Gonna Git You Sucka* in 1988. Chris, the young man from Brooklyn with the big comedy dream, was on his way.

⟫ LATE NIGHT BECKONS ⟪

After giving it a go in Hollywood, Chris Rock seemed ready for his next big step. By 1990 *Saturday Night Live (SNL)* had been a staple of late-night television for 15 years. Many of its regulars, including

A promotional poster for Eddie Murphy's 1987 action-comedy *Beverly Hills Cop II*. When Murphy saw Chris's stand-up act, he was impressed and offered Chris a small role in the film. Chris played a parking valet in his big-screen debut. He gained valuable show business experience, and he also developed a lasting friendship with Murphy.

The cast of NBC's popular comedy program *Saturday Night Live*, September 1992. Pictured are (front row, left to right) Chris Farley, Al Franken, and Melanie Hutsell; (second row) Chris Rock, Julia Sweeney, Dana Carvey, and Rob Schneider; (third row) Adam Sandler, David Spade, Ellen Cleghorne, Kevin Nealon, Phil Hartman, and Tim Meadows.

Murphy, Bill Murray, Chevy Chase, and John Belushi, had gone on to become big stars. Appearing on one of the funniest shows on network television often led to movie roles and product advertising deals. At the very least, it could make comedic actors well known.

Based on his growing list of credits and a recommendation from Murphy, Chris landed an audition for *SNL* with producer Lorne Michaels. Chris got the job and still considers it a turning point in his career:

CROSS-CURRENTS

For the history of one of the most famous and successful comedy programs, read "Lorne Michaels and Saturday Night Live." Go to page 49. ▶▶

❝ 'Saturday Night Live' was the best time of my life. It was like X-Men School for comedians. When Lorne Michaels shook my hand, I haven't been broke since. I never smelled broke again since I met Lorne Michaels. ❞

Chris's work on *Saturday Night Live* proved disappointing, however. He clearly had talent, but during most broadcasts he was given only background roles. He had few chances to create the sorts of unforgettable characters his idol, Eddie Murphy, had once created. One exception was his character Nat X, an angry **black power** supporter. It was an artistically difficult time for Chris, but he was able to continue working the comedy clubs, something he clearly loved. His first comedy album, *Born Suspect*, was released in 1991 to modest success. He stayed on a similar track with his 1997 book, *Rock This!* In it, he writes:

CROSS-CURRENTS

For some background information on Chris's popular character Nat X, check out "History Gets Rocked: Black Power." Go to page 50 ▶▶

❝ Sometimes I hate life because I was born a suspect. All black men are born suspects. When I came out of my mother, right away, if anything happened in a three-block radius, I was a suspect. As a matter of fact, the day I was born, somebody's car got stolen from the hospital parking lot. They made me stand in a lineup. ❞

⟫ WHAT NOW? ⟪

Film work also continued, including an acclaimed role as a drug addict in *New Jack City*. Still, Chris's frustration with *SNL* grew. He was convinced he could be more successful away from the show and left in 1993. Immediately afterward he was hired as "special guest" on the popular Fox variety show *In Living Color*, but the show was canceled soon after. Although Chris decided to return to film, his hilarious but commercially unsuccessful 1993 rap spoof, *CB4*, took him nowhere. By 1995 it looked as though his show-business career would be brief unless something drastically changed.

The DVD cover of Chris's 1996 stand-up special, *Bring the Pain*. In a 2004 interview, Chris recalled that before the HBO special aired, he was afraid that his career was faltering. He therefore approached *Bring the Pain* as his one big chance to say something relevant. The special was very successful, putting Chris back into the spotlight.

The Bad with the Good

FROM THE BEGINNING OF HIS CAREER, CHRIS Rock's greatest talent had been for stand-up comedy performances. And although his first HBO comedy special in 1994 had won him some fans, it was his return to the stage in 1996's *Bring the Pain* that brought his young career back to life.

The special won two Emmys, but more importantly Chris found his voice, with a foul-mouthed **tirade** against white America, black America, and personal relationships. The racial divide between blacks and whites continued to be comedic gold for Chris, as it would be throughout his career.

In interviews, Chris is often questioned about his views on race. One writer asked Chris his opinion about the African-American experience. Chris's response was predictably funny yet also honest:

CROSS-CURRENTS

To find out about other mocumentaries like Chris's film CB4, read "Music Spoofs: Spinal Tap and A Mighty Wind." Go to page 50. ▶▶

> **"**I am African American, so whatever experience I am going through is the African American experience. If I decided to go to Antarctica and raise polar bears, it's still the African American experience. Should I lift people up? Everyone, black or white, should feel a responsibility to help others.**"**

➤ A SHOW TO CALL HIS OWN ➤

The success of the stand-up show proved to HBO executives that Chris Rock was more popular than ever before. In 1996 the network asked him to produce and host *The Chris Rock Show*, a cross between his rapid-fire stand-up routines and *Saturday Night Live*. It was an opportunity to be front and center in a **sketch comedy** show, one that featured his one-of-a-kind, uncensored take on the world. *The Chris Rock Show* also included a talk-show element, in which Chris sat behind a desk and spoke with a variety of interesting personalities, such as basketball star Allen Iverson or model and actor Tyson Beckford. Musical guests, including Mary J. Blige and Method Man, also appeared on the show. Acting as ringmaster was Chris himself, with his unique brand of racially charged humor. The taped bits ranged from man-on-the-street interviews to sketch comedy—the kind he had rarely gotten a chance to do on *Saturday Night Live*.

In one episode, Chris visited the mostly white town of Howard Beach in Queens, New York, and asked citizens to sign a petition in favor of changing the name of a local street, Cross Bay Boulevard, to Tupac Shakur Boulevard. The gangsta rapper had been murdered a few years before; his reputation among older whites was particularly controversial, to say the least. Chris's cameras captured the stunned—and sometimes angry—looks on people's faces as he asked them to support his idea.

Race was also the subject of a 2000 episode in which Chris Rock stood before a chart to discuss the strides and setbacks African Americans had experienced during their history in the United States.

> **"**You hear black people say 'We're almost there' . . . but every time we've made strides we've been offset by missteps . . . in 1960, SNCC [the Student Nonviolent Coordinating Committee, a civil-rights group] staged sit-ins, putting us ahead four steps.

A DVD collection of *The Chris Rock Show*, which combined celebrity interviews with stand-up and sketch comedy. The program ran for three seasons on HBO, from 1997 to 2000. It won an Emmy Award in 1999 for Outstanding Writing for a Variety or Music Program. Chris's writing collaborators included fellow comedians Louis C.K. and Wanda Sykes.

But in 1988, the Crips and Bloods staged shoot-outs, putting black people six steps back, and six feet under. **"**

The Chris Rock Show continued in this comic vein. It mixed utter silliness—like the fake afterschool special "Daddy Still Has a Flattop," in which a kid is embarrassed by his pop's haircut—with smart jokes ripped from the front pages of the day's newspapers. Were these bits also Chris's way of making a serious statement about what he believed to be the state of African American life in the new century? When asked such questions in interviews, Chris denies any hidden motives and says he is only telling jokes.

➤ INFLUENCES AND ADJUSTMENTS ◀

Despite his denials, comedy—particularly comedy performed by black comedians—has often done more for audiences than simply make them laugh. Chris Rock's joke-telling heroes include Rodney Dangerfield, Sam Kinison, George Carlin, and Richard Pryor. Pryor—who like Chris is African American—made his name during the late 1960s and early 1970s as a brash and bold funnyman. But Pryor's side-splitting observations on blacks and whites in America were also cutting and barely hid the pain of **discrimination** known to so many African Americans.

Some in the media have criticized Chris because they believe he makes fun of race in his routines. Others have come to his defense by saying that racially charged comedy helps people from different backgrounds better understand each other. Either way, during its three-year run *The Chris Rock Show* remained popular because Chris refused to play it safe.

In return, Chris Rock's show won a slew of Emmys and influenced a new generation of sketch comedians, including the popular Dave Chappelle, whose Comedy Central series exploded onto the scene in 2003. Chris spoke about his sudden fame to *Jet* magazine in 1997:

"It's beyond my wildest expectations . . . I think I finally got my act together.

I don't believe in 'You've been working this long and this is supposed to happen to you.' It's art; it is not a factory, meaning, it happens when you're good. In most cases, the longer you do something, the better you get, but I just think I am doing better work than I've ever done. **"**

Yet the show could be a grind for Chris. He maintained complete control of the program's material—the first time, aside from his stand-up, that this had happened—but he did not want to be tied down. Therefore, he jumped at other opportunities, such as appearing on the popular Fox sitcom *Martin*, starring Martin Lawrence, and in the occasional dramatic role as he did on *Homicide: Life on the Street*.

On September 14, 1997, Chris poses with the two Emmy Award statuettes that he won for his HBO stand-up special *Bring the Pain*. Some of the most controversial lines of Chris's career were part of his *Bring the Pain* show. Chris later feared that the special's most famous routine could be misinterpreted as approving of racism.

The few movie roles offered to him—in 1996's *Sgt. Bilko* and 1997's *Beverly Hills Ninja*—hardly showed what Chris could do. Although he was doing well enough financially, Chris Rock had yet to find his place in the acting world. Movie studios, it seemed, did not know what to do with him.

➤ STAYING UP AND SETTLING DOWN ◄

Regardless of his career struggles, Chris's personal life was about to take a new turn. As his celebrity had grown in the late 1980s and early 1990s, Chris Rock was often photographed with a beautiful starlet or model. In his act, he often spoke about the challenges of romantic relationships and the pitfalls of commitment.

But one girlfriend, Malaak Compton, was different from other women he had dated. Not only was she a gorgeous, dark-haired beauty, she was also bright and had an interest in business. They met at a New York City awards show in 1994. After a two-year courtship, they married on November 23, 1996.

Marriage apparently agreed with Chris, as personal happiness and professional notice came quickly. In 1998 Chris landed a coveted role in *Lethal Weapon 4*. This latest in the series of Mel Gibson/Danny Glover cops-and-robbers blockbusters gave Chris a chance to show off a version of his stand-up routine. Chris had some of the movie's best lines and got to work with Gibson, one of the biggest box-office stars of the 1990s. *Lethal Weapon 4* marked Chris's first true box-office success.

On the heels of that movie came voice work in the Eddie Murphy remake of *Doctor Dolittle*. The reunion of the two African-American comedians after more than a decade proved to be a good move. Chris provided the voice of a guinea pig named Rodney, who speaks to Murphy's character, Dr. John Dolittle. The 1998 comedy film proved to be box-office gold, earning more than $100 million.

At this point, though, Chris was careful to remain loyal to adult audiences. In 1999 he played a tough-talking, foul-mouthed character in the film *Dogma*, a satire on religious faith in the modern day. His character was Rufus, the 13th apostle, who had been left out of the New Testament because he was black. The movie proved controversial, as a number of religious groups protested that its content was offensive.

His next movie role, 2000's *Nurse Betty*, teamed Chris with Oscar-winner Morgan Freeman. The two played cold-blooded killers

Chris's wife, Malaak Compton-Rock was born in Oakland, California, and graduated from Howard University. She worked as a public relations executive, organizing celebrity fundraisers to benefit the United Nations children's aid fund UNICEF. Now, she devotes herself to charitable work on a full-time basis. Chris often lends his support to her efforts.

on the run, and this time Chris had a chance to play both comedy and drama. He threw himself into the role of Wesley with delight. Although the film received mixed reviews and was not a box-office success, Chris was not sure that mattered. He was finally being offered interesting movie roles that he could sink his teeth into.

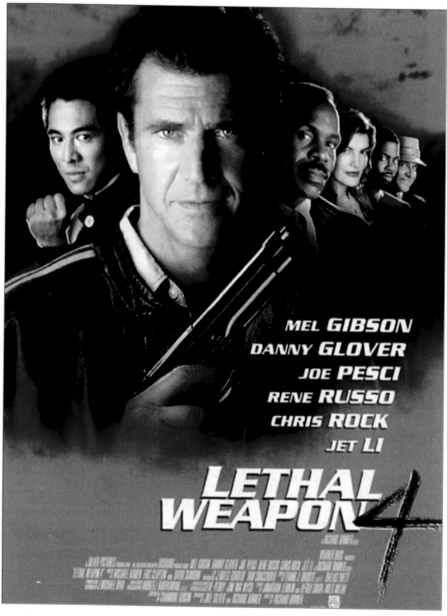

Lethal Weapon 4 was an important boost for Chris's acting career. In a memorable supporting role, Chris played a wisecracking police detective who investigates an immigrant smuggling ring alongside sergeants portrayed by Danny Glover and Mel Gibson. The 1998 action-comedy was a big hit, earning more than $285 million in theaters worldwide.

⧳ FADE TO BLACK ⧳

In between life on the film set, Chris went on the road again. By now he had a routine for developing his jokes for live audiences. First, he would collect all of the new jokes and observations he had written. Then, he would give a series of performances across the country where he could test out the material—see what worked and what did not—and make the adjustments he felt necessary to "kill" the crowd every night. Such work could take months of shaping and honing like a sculptor before he was satisfied.

By the time his new HBO special—now titled *Bigger and Blacker*—made the air, Chris had a hilarious home run on his hands. In the three years since *Bring the Pain*, Chris had hardly mellowed. If anything, the 34-year-old comedian had become sharper and tougher. He stalked the stage like a panther in a black leather suit. Microphone in hand, his voice a high-pitched screech, Chris held forth on murdered rap stars, the state of black leadership, and what women want.

While some critics suggested that Chris sacrificed good taste for cheap and, sometimes, insulting laughs, audiences gobbled it up. He played to sold-out houses across the country, and millions tuned in to watch him on HBO. Some observers even noted a touch of the old-time, Bible-thumping evangelist in his delivery. Chris agreed, citing family history:

> **❝I'm from like a family of preachers. My dad broke the mold and then I continued to break the mold. I grew up a lot around preachers. And I guess some of it gets into the work. ❞**

Striking a balance between movies, his HBO television show, and his new marriage proved a challenge, but Chris was determined to forge a versatile career that offered him a wide variety of opportunities. Only one question remained: What next?

As Chris Rock's film and television career continued
to expand, he decided to branch out into writing and
producing mainstream movies. His projects met with
mixed success, but all were generally recognized as
interesting. Chris has said that while he will continue
exploring his filmmaking interest, he still considers
himself first and foremost a stand-up comedian.

Taking Control

DESPITE CHRIS ROCK'S SUCCESS, HIS EDGY humor still had its critics. In a June 2001 article in *New Republic* magazine, writer Justin Driver spoke of being less than thrilled by Rock and another African American comedian, Chris Tucker, a star of the *Rush Hour* series of movies. He saw Rock and Tucker as shameless promoters of black cultural stereotypes.

Driver compared the two comedians to the 1920s movie actor Stepin Fetchit. During Hollywood's early years, Stepin Fetchit played a series of black characters who were lazy, stupid, and subservient to others. Furthermore, wrote Driver, neither Rock nor Tucker could be compared to other black comic geniuses, such as Richard Pryor:

> **"**[Rock and Tucker] are attempting to shuck, jive, grin, shout, and bulge their eyes all the way back to the

CROSS-CURRENTS

To learn more about one of the most famous racial stereotypes in the history of Hollywood, read "Stepin Fetchit." Go to page 51. ▶▶

days of minstrelsy. . . . Rock's comedy is divided
against itself by a stark and unfortunate contrast
in content and form. . . . When [Richard] Pryor riffed
on the differences between blacks and whites—
between, say, black funerals and white funerals—
a measure of courage was required. **"**

The suggestion that Chris Rock's comedy lacked courage stung. But Chris typically shrugs off such criticism. Like many comics before him, he often walks a fine line between insight and offense. But more times than not, he dismisses the line altogether, firing off his thoughts on racism, the state of black America, drugs, and marriage like a flamethrower. In Chris Rock's brand of comedy, everything is fair game. Well, not quite everything. When asked if there is something or someone he would never make fun of, he cites television host Oprah Winfrey. His reason: There are so few black billionaires, he does not want to offend one.

⇒ EARTHLY MATTERS ⇐

After *The Chris Rock Show* ended in 2000, the comedian returned to movies. He was also taking a larger role in writing and producing projects. In 2001 came *Down to Earth*. Chris cowrote the film—a remake—with three others, including old friend and comedian Louis C.K. The story of a man pulled from an accident before his time by a misguided angel and transplanted into another body clearly had comic potential. In fact, *Down to Earth* was the third version of the tale. The first was 1941's *Here Comes Mr. Jordan*, which won several Oscars. It was followed in 1978 by *Heaven Can Wait*, which starred Warren Beatty and Julie Christie.

Third times are often the charm, but the Rock version—with Chris as Lance Barton, a failed comedian put into the body of a rich white guy—received a drubbing from the critics. A few thought it too safe, too willing to play for easy racial laughs, such as the rich man, inhabited by Barton's spirit, suddenly becoming a fan of rap music. Although the movie fared poorly both critically and at the box office, Chris's interest in remaking older films and putting a new spin on them would continue.

That same year, Chris bounced into the animated comedy *Osmosis Jones* and performed in director Kevin Smith's *Jay and Silent Bob*

CHRIS ROCK

DOWN TO EARTH

Chris's first lead role in a movie was in 2001's *Down to Earth*, as an amateur stand-up comedian whose spirit lands in the body of an older, wealthy white man. Chris's co-stars included Regina King as his love interest, and Eugene Levy as a clumsy angel. Chris also worked on the screenplay, which was based on several earlier films.

Strike Back. This was the second time that Chris had worked with Smith, an award-winning director; previously they had collaborated on *Dogma.* Another popular director, Steven Spielberg, even hired Chris to provide a voice in his science-fiction tale *Artificial Intelligence: AI.*

Chris felt most comfortable working with old friends. Along with comedian and actress Wanda Sykes, he played multiple roles in *Pootie Tang,* written and directed by pal Louis C.K. Considered a cult classic by some fans, the movie revolves around the title character, a movie-star superhero played by Lance Crouther. With his bizarre speech and a blistering, whip-cracking belt that he uses to defend himself, Pootie is a sweet-natured and lovable character. The movie is a silly tribute to blaxploitation movies of the 1960s and 1970s. Chris had grown up watching such flicks as *Superfly, Shaft,* and *Watermelon Man.* Now he had the chance to poke fun at them using his own twisted sense of humor.

⮞ FAMILY MAN ⮜

Chris put his movie career on hold briefly when his wife, Malaak, gave birth to a daughter, Lola Simone, on June 28, 2002. Fatherhood gave Chris the perfect excuse to take a break and refocus his showbiz work. He made only one movie in 2002, the cop film *Bad Company* with British actor Anthony Hopkins.

The opportunity to work with Hopkins, an Oscar winner best known for playing demonic serial killer Hannibal Lecter in the 1991 thriller *Silence of the Lambs,* was too hard for Chris to pass up. But the pairing of the elegant Brit and the straight-talking American, as good guys fighting nuclear terrorists, never took flight. *Bad Company* failed with critics and movie fans alike, earning barely $30 million in movie theaters. Most critics cited poor direction and a lackluster script that gave neither actor much to do.

Finding good film scripts was a common problem in Hollywood, especially for young black actors such as Chris Rock. Few good roles were being written for people of color. The movie scripts that Chris did receive all followed a similar racial pattern, as he tells interviewer Larry King:

❝ **Right now, where I am in Hollywood, I get the scripts after Eddie Murphy, Will Smith, Martin**

Lawrence, Chris Tucker. You know how bad the scripts I get must be? Typical script is I rob people, some illegal activity. . . . And I'm not even good at doing the illegal activity. . . . Then I meet a white man, and he shows me the light! Thank God for Whitey!"

Although he had to laugh at the predictable material he was being offered, he also understood the history of black actors. For years movie roles for African Americans were typically limited to butlers and maids, drugs dealers, or pimps. Actresses such as

This promotional poster for the spy movie *Bad Company* features Anthony Hopkins and Chris Rock. The film, about a terrorist plot to attack New York city, had been scheduled for release in November 2001. However, after real terrorists attacked New York on September 11, 2001, the movie's release was delayed until June 2002.

Gone with the Wind's Hattie McDaniel and *Carmen Jones*'s Dorothy Dandridge proved that black actors were just as capable as white ones. Yet long after these two women left the spotlight, people of color remained **typecast**. Few had broken free of Hollywood's narrow-minded views on race. But some did. Photographer Gordon Parks directed the popular 1970s film *Shaft*, and actor Sidney Poitier virtually created the image of the strong and intelligent black man on-screen. More recently, Denzel Washington has spun box-office gold by playing a wide variety of characters, including a gangster, a teacher, a Civil War soldier, and a corrupt cop.

CROSS-CURRENTS

If you would like more information about a groundbreaking African American movie actress, read "Dorothy Dandridge." Go to page 52. ▶▶

⇒ ROCKING THE DIRECTOR'S CHAIR ⇐

By early 2003 Chris Rock clearly had a shot at long-term stardom. He had already written movies and television shows, but for his next project Chris took another leap of faith: directing. For a man with such strong opinions, it was the natural next step, and the subject of *Head of State* seemed perfect for Chris's own unique brand of humor. Chris starred as Mays Gilliam, a local Washington, D.C., politician suddenly thrust into the spotlight upon the death of a 2004 presidential candidate and his running mate. Gilliam is then drafted to run for the highest office in the land. The story provided Chris the chance to play with racial politics—something he had done in his stage act for so many years. It also allowed him to live out his boyhood dream of being president of the United States. As his sidekick and vice-presidential candidate, Chris hired comedian Bernie Mac.

According to Chris, the idea had been in his head for years. Although he had directing in mind early on, studio executives either told him he was not ready yet or, as he claims, said he was not smart enough. But when the movie got the green light from the movie company, Chris jumped at the chance for almost complete creative control.

Released in March 2003, *Head of State* marked a new and exciting chapter in the life and career of Chris Rock. In a 1996 routine, he had jokingly claimed that a black man would never become vice president, let alone reach the presidency. Now Chris was making the impossible

Chris accepts a star on the Hollywood Walk of Fame in Los Angeles on March 12, 2003. Celebrities receive stars to acknowledge their contributions to the entertainment industry. Family members were there to celebrate as well. Chris's wife Malaak and daughter Lola are pictured on the left, and his mother Rose and brother Tony are on the right.

possible, at least on film. Best efforts aside, though, *Head of State* earned mixed reviews. One reviewer noted in *Entertainment Weekly*,

> **The rhythms are all over the place in *Head of State*, and not all of them are steady; Rock is most prone to stumbling when he tries to shoehorn stand-alone, stand-up lines into the action. . . . More valuably, though, Rock, one of the most astute**

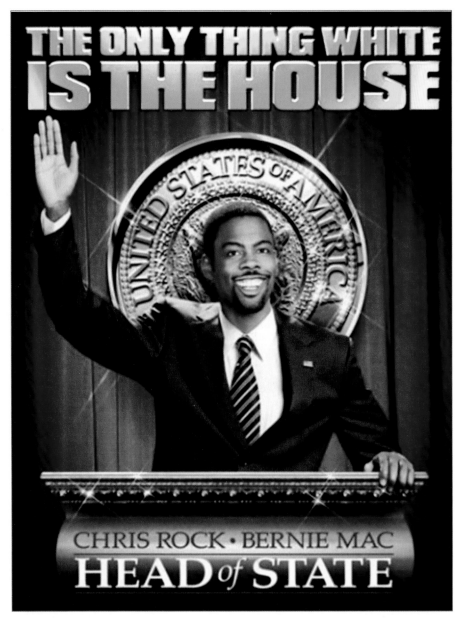

THE ONLY THING WHITE IS THE HOUSE

UNITED STATES OF AMERICA

CHRIS ROCK · BERNIE MAC
HEAD *of* STATE

Chris says his inspiration for the movie *Head of State*—in which a political party nominates a black candidate for president to help its image, not expecting him to win—came partly from the election of 1984. In that historic election, the Democratic Party nominated a woman, Geraldine Ferraro, as its vice-presidential candidate.

comic talents working today, revels in impassioned commentary about the state of American politics and race relations, all imparted with a grin [and] a twinkle. **"**

The box-office earnings for *Head of State* were respectable—enough to ensure Chris another crack behind the camera. But for many moviegoers, the comic payoffs of a black presidency never came through. Regardless, Chris Rock had done it his way. The pride and satisfaction he got from putting the pieces together himself made up for the film's lukewarm response.

➤ FAMILY MAN II ◀

Little more than a year later, Chris found another reason to be proud as his wife gave birth to the couple's second child. The two welcomed daughter Zahra Savannah on May 22, 2004. Shortly before the arrival of Lola, two years earlier, the Rocks had picked up and moved out of Brooklyn and into the New Jersey suburb of Alpine. The quest for better schools, a better neighborhood, and a piece of land to call their own allowed the family to remain close to New York City. But at age 38, Chris was intent on truly setting down.

When questioned, the comedian will say little about his home life. Still, when on the road and close to home, he sometimes hires a driver to take him up (or down) the New Jersey turnpike late at night after a gig. He loves being home in the morning to make the kids breakfast and get them off to school. And like almost everything else in his life, he rarely passes up the opportunity to make a joke out of it. He recently quipped to British talk-show host Jonathan Ross about raising his children differently than he was raised:

" They're rich kids, and the weird thing is, no matter what I do my kids are like rich kids. And I've never *liked* rich kids. So there's a part of me that actually hates my own children. **"**

This image is part of an advertising campaign for a clothing line with a twist. Some of the money earned from sales of the clothing is donated to help people in Africa, particularly those suffering from the impact of HIV or AIDS. Throughout his career Chris has used his celebrity to help people who are less fortunate.

5

Comedy Legend in the Making

KIDS, RICH OR OTHERWISE, WOULD FIGURE EVEN more prominently in Chris Rock's work beginning in 2005. One of his many projects was a television show about his hard-knock life as a Brooklyn elementary school student. *Everybody Hates Chris*, narrated by Chris himself, features a family much like his own, but with a healthy dose of exaggeration.

The title—a play on the popular comedy series *Everybody Loves Raymond*—suited Chris's ironic sense of humor; but unlike much of his past work, the show was aimed at families. Although Chris could never be accused of being wholesome, *Everybody Hates Chris* is softer and sunnier, relying on characters and relationships rather than pure outrageousness. And if audiences look closely enough, says executive producer Ali LeRoi, they might even detect a hint of message:

"In this era of minority [families] and African Americans where no father is present in the family,

we wanted to go, 'No, these guys are out there.' There are hardworking guys out there who love their wives and love their kids and do anything they can to hold things together. **"**

The show's creator, producer, and narrator is just such a guy. With two children at home, Chris took to expanding his audience. He was working, too, on an animated feature film that he hoped would be a hit. But first came the Oscars.

⋙ GOLDEN OPPORTUNITY ⋘

First held in 1927, the Academy Awards has a history of failing to nominate many people of color. Although Chris was not the first African American to host the awards, he was clearly a controversial choice. The show's most frequent hosts, such as comedians Bob Hope and Billy Crystal, were hilarious and popular, but neither was on the cutting edge. Chris, on the other hand, forged his career with a tough, rude sense of humor. Chris's performance at the Oscars offered the kind of humor audiences have come to expect from him.

Although he might not be invited back, he made his appearance memorable.

The same year that Chris lit up the Kodak Theatre in Los Angeles, *Everybody Hates Chris* premiered to some of the best reviews of Rock's career. Also, DreamWorks Animation asked him to be involved in an animated film. For years, Chris had mostly avoided making movies for children, and at first an offer to do *Madagascar* was no different. But his old friend Eddie Murphy had revived his fading career by voicing the donkey in the *Shrek* movies. Chris claims that when Murphy told him the size of his paycheck, he changed his mind about doing animation.

CROSS-CURRENTS

To learn more about the first African American to host the Academy Awards ceremony, read "Whoopi Goldberg." Go to page 53. ▶▶

⋙ ANIMAL PLANET ⋘

The script for *Madagascar*, about four animal friends in the Central Park Zoo who end up on the **lemur**-filled east African island of the title, was a hoot. Chris's friend Ben Stiller signed on to play the pampered lion, Alex; David Schwimmer played the giraffe, Melman; and Jada Pinkett Smith played the self-loving hippo, Gloria. Rock, in

Chris himself guest-starred in this episode of *Everybody Hates Chris*, playing a school guidance counselor. Tyler James Williams (left) portrays Chris as a teenager. On the show, Chris must deal with strict parents, bickering younger siblings, and a mostly white school. Chris also narrates the show, which was inspired by his memories of growing up in the Bedford-Stuyvesant neighborhood of Brooklyn.

the role of Marty, played a zebra who wants only to roam free on the African plain. The juicy role allowed Chris to shine, as Marty and Alex come to understand their different places in the food chain.

The character of Marty seemed custom made for Chris. The zebra, brave but impulsive, was an awful lot like the brash comedian who voiced him. Chris melted into the role like few others he had been given. The cast, including Sacha Baron Cohen as a goofy lemur king, helped *Madagascar* open big. It was Chris's biggest movie success yet, eventually earning more than $500 million at the box office worldwide.

Madagascar **costars Ben Stiller and Chris Rock pose for photographs at a promotional event for the movie in June 2005. They hold toy versions of their characters, Alex the lion and Marty the zebra. Since** *Madagascar* **became a hit, Chris has done other animated children's films. He voiced a mosquito in 2007's** *Bee Movie* **and committed to a** *Madagascar* **sequel.**

Never one to slow down, Chris immediately began planning his next move: a remake of the classic French film *Chloe in the Afternoon*. While he and writing partner Louis C.K. worked on the script, Chris filmed *The Longest Yard* with friend and former *Saturday Night Live* star Adam Sandler. Centered on a prison football team, the movie was a remake of a well-regarded 1975 film starring Burt Reynolds. *The Longest Yard* made more than $190 million worldwide, and earned Chris a BET Comedy Award for Outstanding Supporting Actor.

☀ LOVE LIFE ☀

The year 2006 was a quiet one for Chris Rock. He mostly stayed out of the public eye, spending time with his family and continuing work on what would be his second directing effort. The plot centered on a married man tempted into an affair with a beautiful and available old friend. *I Think I Love My Wife*, released in 2007, was Chris's attempt at comedy in the vein of one of his heroes, Woody Allen. Allen began as a comedy writer in the 1950s, then moved on to stand-up and, eventually, movies. From his early films to his later work, starting with 1977's multiple Oscar-winner *Annie Hall*, Allen's movies had a major impact on Chris's comic understanding. Chris's new film would be less broad and rely instead on character conflicts.

In *I Think I Love My Wife*, Chris and costar Gina Torres play a couple whose stable but dull marriage is seriously tested. Although some critics complimented the movie's frankness, it was not very successful. The movie was criticized for, among other issues, not properly balancing its realistic subject matter with its slapstick comedy.

In his stand-up routines, Chris often spoke of relationships and the challenges of remaining faithful. This new movie was an attempt to express those ideas in a more sophisticated way, much as Allen did. Billed as the work of "writer-director" Chris Rock, *I Think I Love My Wife* was the comedian's stab at earning greater respect. Disappointingly, though, Chris's baby bombed, earning only $12 million and drawing mostly poor reviews. Many critics remained puzzled that such a talent as Chris Rock was unable to find a movie role that showed his best side.

Meanwhile, *Everybody Hates Chris* was well into its third season and humming along. Chris also took some time to explore his charitable side. For years the funnyman had worked with education and health organizations like **UNICEF** and the Salvation Army. Now he vowed to expand his reach. In early 2007 he attended the opening of the Oprah Winfrey school for girls in South Africa. Later, in a show of his political engagement, he attended a star-studded benefit for Illinois senator Barack Obama's presidential campaign.

⇒ MRS. ROCK HAS STYLE ⇐

Since they were married in 1996, Chris and his wife, Malaak Compton-Rock, have become a well-known and influential couple in Hollywood. Just as Chris works for his favorite causes, Malaak also strives to better the world. In October 1999 she founded styleWORKS, a nonprofit organization dedicated to helping women better themselves as they move from government-funded welfare to work.

At the core of styleWORKS is Malaak's belief that women who feel better about themselves are more likely to get and keep good jobs and take better care of their children. For women with little work experience, styleWORKS offers a free session on hair, makeup, clothing, and interview tips. The goal is to prepare women for job interviews by helping with their professional appearance. According to its Web site, styleWORKS has helped prepare more than 1,000 women for the workplace. More recently, Malaak has appeared as a judge on the television show *Oprah's Big Give*, which strives to help people in need around the country.

⇒ DIVIDE AND CONQUER ⇐

In 2007 Chris began writing new material. He was itching to return to his first love, stand-up comedy. His sold out *No Apologies* tour

Chris attends the New York City premier of *Bee Movie* on October 25, 2007, with his wife Malaak Compton-Rock and their daughters Lola (then age five) and Zahra (then age three). Since becoming a husband and father, Chris has incorporated jokes about the ups and downs of family life into his routines.

began on New Year's Eve 2007 in front of 20,000 rabid fans at New York City's Madison Square Garden. Chris had been refining the routine for months, and he had a lot to say—about President George W. Bush, about Hillary Clinton, and about Barack Obama. Obama, in particular, excited Chris:

> **"Barack Obama—he's a black man with two black names! Barack. Obama. He doesn't let his blackness sneak up on you. As soon as you hear Barack Obama you wonder, 'Does he have a spear?' . . . He's so cool, too, man. I don't think he realizes he's a black candidate!"**

CROSS-CURRENTS

For more information about the 2008 presidential race, read "Barack Obama and the Politics of Race." Go to page 54. ▶▶

More than ever, Chris was in tune with what was going on in the world. Clearly, the 2008 presidential election weighed heavily on him. Concerns about the world his daughters would inherit were on his mind. But the change in his comic content was also matched by a shift in how he performed. Critics noticed this different approach, recognizing that he was as coarse and hilarious as ever, with a twist:

> **"In many ways, the show revealed a new performance style for Rock. He no longer prowled the stage restlessly like a zoo cat, exhorting and challenging the crowd in a street preacher's cadence. Instead, he seemed lighter, less intense, with a more traditional stand-up approach . . . he nonetheless employed a more physical brand of comedy, bolstering his punch lines with gestures and movements."**

No Apologies also marked a departure for Chris in terms of audience. In years past he had played a handful of performances overseas. But **agents** and managers often doubted Chris's ability to score with international audiences. For his part, Chris longed to take his comedy around the world and broaden his audience. In 2008 he booked performances in Great Britain and traveled as far away from home as New Zealand and Australia. Each of the shows quickly sold out.

In between shows, or during the days, Chris was hard at work revisiting one of his most popular characters, Marty the Zebra, for *Madagascar: Escape 2 Africa.* He expected the November 2008 release to score him a holiday-season hit.

⇒ HIS MOMENT ⇐

Chris Rock's next move was less certain. For more than 20 years, the wise-cracking and knowing comedian has forged an extremely varied career that has taken him from comedy clubs to television to movies and back again. He has displayed a rare talent not only as a funnyman but also as an actor and writer. His directing work has yielded mixed results, yet such work is clearly something he strives to improve.

In a time of uncertainty, Chris's biting sense of humor and clever observations about people, politicians, and race make him more valuable than ever. One of Chris's close friends, music promoter Bill Stephney, thinks the comedian's time is now:

"The times compel him, and he processes it as only he can. His mind and eyes should be donated to science. He doesn't really know the gravity of his own power. It's sort of like the Olympics with him: Every handful of years, there's a Chris Rock moment. And we just happen to be in that hot zone, which has maybe never been hotter."

Oscar Hosting: A Prime Gig

The chance to been seen by a billion people; the chance to poke fun at the world's biggest stars; the chance to hang out at all the fancy after parties. These are just three of the benefits of hosting the Academy Awards. Sure, the monkey suit (tuxedo) is a requirement, and you are bound to be scrutinized and no doubt criticized by thousands of critics around the globe. But being asked is also a sign that you have truly hit the big time. Swashbuckling actor Douglas Fairbanks hosted the first awards ceremony in 1929, but since then most of the hosts have been comics. The all-time champ—legend Bob Hope—did the show 20 times, beginning in 1940. Late-night talk-show host Johnny Carson succeeded Hope and took five turns at the microphone beginning in 1978. The 1990s was the Billy Crystal era, marked by Crystal's filmed spoofs of each year's nominated movies. More recently, daffy comic and talk-show host Ellen DeGeneres and multitalented Steve Martin have introduced the awards, as has *Daily Show* host Jon Stewart.

(Go back to page 6.)

Richard Pryor: Comedy Legend

Few comedians are as widely respected as Richard Pryor. Most comedians today list him as a major influence. It is easy to see why: Pryor exuded a confidence and willingness to speak honestly that set him apart. But Pryor's wit was born out of deep-seated pain. Born in Peoria, Illinois, in December 1940, he was raised in his grandmother's brothel and thus exposed to the harsh realities of adulthood at a young age. He was sexually abused first by a neighbor and, later, by a parish priest. His only escape was the local movie house, where he would sit in the blacks-only area and dream of one day appearing on the big screen.

School was not for him, and Pryor was expelled at 14. He subsequently found work at a local club. Problems with the law only provided more material for his ideas about living as a black man in 1950s America. A two-year term in the U.S. Army gave Pryor a series of performing opportunities. After he left the military he tried out as a singer and piano player. But he could not carry a tune, and he quickly realized his jokes scored big with audiences.

Pryor moved to New York, did stand-up in any clubs that would have him, and found bit parts in television shows. He had been inspired by comedians Bill Cosby and Woody Allen, but Pryor honed his own unique voice.

Widely credited as one of the funniest comedians of all time, Richard Pryor could turn anything—his complicated love life, his struggle with drug addiction, even the accident that nearly killed him—into a joke. But although Pryor made audiences laugh throughout the 1970s and 1980s, his routines also contained hard-hitting social commentary.

movies, including *Stir Crazy*, *Which Way Is Up*, and *Jo Jo Dancer*, and comedy clubs. Some of his best stage work can be seen in the concert films *Richard Pryor Live on the Sunset Strip* and *Live and Smokin'*, among others. His albums sold millions of copies—unheard-of for comedy records—and won five Grammy awards.

But there was also a dark side: Pryor was dogged by drug problems throughout his life. In June 1980, he nearly died when he accidentally set himself on fire while freebasing cocaine. He suffered burns over 50 percent of his body and spent six weeks in a California hospital. As he often did, Pryor later used his personal pain in his comedy act.

Ten years later, Pryor was diagnosed with multiple sclerosis, a chronic disease that damages the nervous system. Yet

His routines were often angrier and dirtier than those of other comics. As he became famous, bigger paydays followed. Pryor spent the rest of his career shifting between despite his many setbacks, Pryor never lost his sense of humor and ability to speak honestly and openly about life's challenges. He died in 2005. (Go back to page 9.) ◀◀

The '80s King of Comedy

By the time he was 15, Eddie Murphy was a comedy club regular, performing dead-on imitations. Soon he attracted the notice of television producers. In 1980, when Murphy was 19, *Saturday Night Live* producer Lorne Michaels cast Murphy as a show regular. In his four seasons on the program, from 1980 to 1984, Murphy burned up the small screen. Sketches like "Mr. Robinson's neighborhood"— a wry, streetwise take on the wholesome Mr. Roger's kid show—brought the house down. So did Murphy's grumpy, cigar-chomping Gumby, and his Speedo-clad, hot tub–loving spoof on "the Godfather of Soul," James Brown.

Hollywood soon beckoned, and throughout the rest of the 1980s Murphy starred in a string of blockbusters. From *48 Hours* to *Trading Places* to *Coming to America*, he displayed a sharp wit and an ability to transform himself into many different characters.

Eddie Murphy accepts a Golden Globe Award for Best Performance by An Actor in a Supporting Role in a Motion Picture for Dreamgirls, *on January 15, 2007. Murphy's Academy Award–nominated performance as a drug-addicted soul singer was a departure from the madcap humor that made him famous, demonstrating that Murphy has dramatic talent as well as comedic.*

Murphy's popularity faded in the early 1990s, but by the middle of the decade he was back. The beginning of the comeback may have been his popular remake of the 1960s comedy *The Nutty Professor*. Critics were not always pleased with his work, but audiences came in droves. Murphy continues making successful movies, including *Shrek* and its sequels. A high point of his acting career came with his 2007 Oscar nomination for the musical *Dreamgirls*. (Go back to page 12.) ◄◄

Lorne Michaels and *Saturday Night Live*

In 1975, producer Lorne Michaels came up with a new kind of late-night television show, one made expressly for grown-ups. The 1975 premiere episode of *Saturday Night Live (SNL)* had comedian George Carlin as its host. Combining comedy sketches and new musical performances each week, Michaels's NBC experiment delivered spoofs on the politics and media of the day and was often roll-in-the-aisles funny. From its beginnings, *SNL* boasted a different kind of viewing experience. It also introduced the country to a young and talented cast of "Not Ready for Prime Time Players." First- and second-season standouts included John Belushi, Chevy Chase, Dan Ackroyd, and Gilda Radner. This group created such classic characters as the Coneheads, the Blues Brothers, and the Wide-enders.

After the departure of the original cast, the show continued. Some seasons were better than others—especially those featuring cast members like Eddie Murphy, Bill Murray, and Billy Crystal, and later Dana Carvey, Phil Hartman, and Mike Myers—and ratings came and went. Yet through all kinds of weather, except for a few years in the 1980s when he left the show, Lorne Michaels kept the *Saturday Night Live* ship afloat. Michaels's 1975 experiment has outlasted the show's critics to become one of the longest-running shows in television history.

(Go back to page 14.) ◀◀

Lorne Michaels, the creator of Saturday Night Live, *has played an important role in the sketch comedy show's success. Since its origin in 1975,* Saturday Night Live *has helped shape popular culture. The show helped launch the careers of many comedians who became major stars, including John Belushi, Bill Murray, Mike Myers, Adam Sandler, Tina Fey, and Chris Rock.*

History Gets Rocked: Black Power

One of Chris Rock's most popular *Saturday Night Live* characters was Nat X. Nat first appeared on November 10, 1990, during Rock's first season on the show. Based on black militant leaders of the 1960s and 1970s, such as Huey Newton and Stokely Carmichael, Nat X wore an afro and an attitude. He would greet guests by rudely telling them to sit down, and then speak at length about a white conspiracy against African Americans.

Chris based the character on a portion of his early stand-up act, and *SNL* audiences loved it. The comedian channeled the extreme ideas and paranoia that resulted from racism against people of color in the United States. During one Nat X skit, he compared the experience of a favorite Christmas character to the black experience:

> **"All the other reindeer used to laugh and call him names. They never let poor Rudolph play in any reindeer games. Rudolph the Red Nosed Reindeer, he wasn't black, but he sure got treated like he was."**

Nat X returned a handful of times during Chris Rock's run on the late-night television show, which ended in 1993.

(Go back to page 15.)

Music Spoofs: *Spinal Tap* and *A Mighty Wind*

The 1984 film *This Is Spinal Tap*, directed by Rob Reiner, claimed to be a documentary about a once-great heavy metal band called Spinal Tap. By the time the movie catches up with the middle-aged rockers, they have seen better musical days. On tour to promote their new album, *Smell the Glove*, Spinal Tap finds its popularity fading. Each concert attracts fewer and fewer fans; fighting within the band puts its future in doubt. Along the way, uproarious moments ensue: Band members get lost on their way to the stage, they play second fiddle to a puppet show, and they have a hard time telling the difference between stupid and clever. Although barely seen when first released, *Spinal Tap* has since become a comedy classic.

Spinal Tap actor Christopher Guest also writes and directs and has made his share of satires. A recent Guest work, *A Mighty Wind*, takes a good-natured swipe at folk music. The deadpan look at once-popular 1960s musicians who stage a reunion tour contains upbeat, Oscar-nominated music and silly situations. In both cases, *This Is Spinal Tap* and *A Mighty Wind* gave audiences a chance to laugh not only at the broad characters and situations on-screen but also at their own love of music.

(Go back to page 17.)

Stepin Fetchit

Lincoln Perry began his acting career in the early 1900s. He took the stage name Stepin Fetchit—a contraction of "Step and Fetch It"—to suggest that the character he played on stage was a servant, willing and able to obey his master. The character Perry played was a version of a common type played by African-American actors in the decades after the American Civil War. Fetchit was slow and lazy, an ugly stereotype that, nonetheless, made audiences—white and black—laugh. But it was only a role. Perry, in fact, was nothing like the character that made him rich and famous. With the introduction of talkies—movies with sound—Perry transformed his stage work into big-screen success, mostly in films with all-black casts.

Perry's career ebbed in the 1930s, and eventually his work came to be seen as degrading and offensive to black people. After Perry's death in 1985, film scholars took another look at his movies. Most of them still view the Stepin Fetchit character as an offensive racial stereotype. But many also recognize Perry's talent for comedy. He made 54 films during his long career and helped lead the way for generations of black actors that followed.

(Go back to page 27.) ◄◄

Lincoln Theodore Perry (right), better known as Stepin Fetchit, performs in the 1938 motion picture His Eventful Night *with costar Charley Ruggles. Perry was a successful actor during the 1920s and 1930s—the first African American actor to become a millionaire. However, the mannerisms of the Stepin Fetchit character upset many black people who were attempting to fight stereotypes.*

Dorothy Dandridge

Dorothy Dandridge was a beautiful and talented African-American actress at a time when few blacks could succeed in Hollywood. Her mother, Ruby, was a working actress who dreamed of making it in the movies. Ruby instilled in her two daughters a love of performing. Dorothy and her sister, Vivian, got work dancing and singing in places like the famed Cotton Club and the Apollo Theater. In 1937 15-year-old Dorothy appeared in her first full-length film, *A Day at the Races*, featuring the Marx Brothers.

Dorothy's movie work was infrequent, and the parts she did get were mostly the stereotypical roles commonly given to actors of color. But in 1954, Dandridge landed the lead in director Otto Preminger's *Carmen Jones*, an all-black version of the opera *Carmen*. The role made Dandridge a star and earned her an Academy Award nomination for Best Actress, the first time an African American had been so honored.

After this, Dorothy's acting opportunities dried up. In those days few parts were written for blacks, even Oscar nominees. By the 1960s Dandridge was making films in Mexico and earning a living by performing on stage, as she had years earlier. She was found dead in her apartment in the fall of 1965, the victim of an accidental drug overdose. Dorothy was only 42 years old.

(Go back to page 32.)

Dorothy Jean Dandridge as the title character in 1954's Carmen Jones. *That role earned her an Academy Award nomination for Best Actress. But even after this honor, it was difficult for Dandridge to find movie work that showcased her musical and acting talent, as opposed to roles that stereotyped African-American women.*

Whoopi Goldberg

The rise of Whoopi Goldberg is an example of how talent and persistence can overcome almost any hardships. Goldberg is one of the few people who have won an Oscar, a Grammy, an Emmy, and a Tony award. Born Caryn Elaine Johnson in New York City in 1955, she created her stage name from a whoopee cushion (*Whoopi*) and from Jewish ancestors (*Goldberg*).

After early independent film work, Goldberg conceived *The Spook Show*, in which she portrayed a series of bizarre yet likeable characters. Famed film and theater director Mike Nichols saw her work and helped her bring it to Broadway, where it ran successfully for 156 performances. Soon after, she received a call from director Steven Spielberg, who later cast her in his film *The Color Purple*, based on the Pulitzer Prize–winning novel by Alice Walker. Goldberg played Celie, an abused woman living in the South during the 1930s. She was nominated for an Oscar for her performance.

A flood of movie roles followed, including *Jumpin' Jack Flash*, *Corinna Corinna*, and an Oscar-winning turn in the romantic drama *Ghost*. In 1994 Goldberg became the first

In 1990, Whoopi Goldberg became the second African-American woman to receive a Best Supporting Actress Oscar, after Hattie McDaniel (who had won in 1939 for Gone with the Wind*). Goldberg won the award for her performance in* Ghost*, as a psychic who communicates with spirits. In 1994, she returned to the Academy Awards stage, this time as the ceremony's host.*

African American and the first woman to be the sole host of the Academy Awards ceremony. She returned to the podium three more times, in 1996, 1999, and 2002.

(Go back to page 38.)

Barack Obama and the Politics of Race

Barack Obama has led a unique American life. His mother was a white student from Kansas, his father an African student from Kenya. Soon after Barack was born in 1961, his father—for whom he is named—returned to his native land, and only visited his son—now living in Honolulu, Hawaii, with his maternal grandparents—only once.

In his memoir, *Dreams from My Father*, Obama writes of his early life in Hawaii as well as his move to Jakarta, Indonesia, after his mother remarried. Race was an unavoidable fact of life for this biracial young man, and from an early age he identified himself as African American. After completing his bachelor's degree at Columbia University in New York, he landed a job as a community organizer in Chicago. The pay was not good, but Obama had a chance to work for things he believed in: better housing for the poor and fairer wages for the average worker. In 1988 he met Michelle Robinson while working at a Chicago law firm for the summer. They would marry in 1992. He also returned to school—Harvard—for his law degree. While there he became the first black editor of the prestigious *Harvard Law Review*. His growing reputation earned him a book contract, a part-time job teaching law, and a position as a civil-rights attorney.

In 1997 he was elected to the Illinois General Assembly, where he spent the next seven years. He lost a campaign for the U.S. House of Representatives in 2000, but by 2003 he had his sights set on a new goal: the U.S. Senate. By Election Day 2004 he was well known beyond the borders of Illinois, thanks to a speech he gave at the 2004 Democratic National Convention in Boston. Obama's poise and speaking ability helped him win the senate seat with 70 percent of the vote.

As a senator, Obama opposed the Iraq War and voiced his support for energy independence and health-care reform. After much discussion with family and advisers, in early 2007 Obama announced that he would seek the presidency at the Old State Capitol building in Springfield, Illinois.

At first, Obama's candidacy was a long shot. His main opponent in the Democratic Party's primary, Senator Hillary Rodham Clinton, was better known and had more money. But hard campaigning and organizing kept him in the hunt when other Democratic candidates fell away. In the summer of 2008, Obama made history by becoming the first African American nominated for president by a major political party.

(Go back to page 44.)

Although Chris Rock is usually quiet about his political views, he publicly pledged his support to Barack Obama's groundbreaking bid for the presidency in 2008. In one June 2008 speech, speaking about personal responsibility, Obama mentioned a Chris Rock comedy routine in which the comedian mocks people who brag about minimal accomplishments, like staying out of jail.

1965   Christopher Julius Rock III is born in Andrews, South Carolina. Soon after, his family moves to New York.

1987   Rock is discovered by superstar Eddie Murphy while doing his routine in a comedy club. Murphy casts the young comic in his film *Beverly Hills Cop II*.

1990   After more bit parts in a series of movies, Rock lands a job on *Saturday Night Live*.

1991   Rock is praised for his portrayal of a crack addict in the film *New Jack City*.

1993   Rock spends his last season on *SNL* before leaving to pursue a life in stand-up and movies; writes and stars in the mocumentary film *CB4*.

1996   Rock tapes *Bring the Pain* for HBO and is hailed as a comedian on the rise. He marries Malaak Compton.

1997   Rock begins writing and starring in *The Chris Rock Show* for HBO. The show runs for three seasons.

1998   Rock is cast in the Mel Gibson/Danny Glover movie *Lethal Weapon 4*; voices a character in *Dr. Dolittle* with Eddie Murphy.

2001   Rock tapes his second hit HBO special, *Bigger and Blacker*. He releases *Down to Earth*, which he writes and stars in.

2002   Rock's daughter, Lola Simone, is born on June 28, 2002.

2003   He directs his first film, *Head of State*, about a black man who runs for president of the United States.

2004   A second child, daughter Zahra Savannah, is born on May 22, 2004.

2005   Rock hosts the Academy Awards; narrates a hit television series, *Everybody Hates Chris*; and stars in the animated film *Madagascar*, which earns more than $500 million at the box office.

2007   Rock directs his second film, *I Think I Love My Wife*.

2008   Rock returns to the road with his *No Apologies* tour on New Year's Eve. He also stars in the sequel *Madagascar: Escape 2 Africa*.

Awards

1997 Emmy Award/Outstanding Variety, Music or Comedy Special for *Chris Rock: Bring the Pain*

1999 Blockbuster Entertainment Award/Favorite Supporting Actor—Action/Adventure for *Lethal Weapon 4*

Emmy Award/Outstanding Writing for a Variety or Music Program for *The Chris Rock Show*

2000 American Comedy Award/Funniest Male Performer in a TV Special (Leading or Supporting) Network, Cable, or Syndication for *Chris Rock: Bigger and Blacker*

2005 BET Comedy Award/Outstanding Supporting Actor in a Theatrical Film for *The Longest Yard*

2006 Kids' Choice Award/Favorite Voice from an Animated Feature for *Madagascar*

Movies and Television

1987 *Beverly Hills Cop II*
Miami Vice

1988 *I'm Gonna Git You Sucka*

1991 *New Jack City*

1992 *Boomerang*

1993 *CB4*

1990–93 *Saturday Night Live*

1993–94 *In Living Color*

1995 *The Fresh Prince of Bel-Air*
The Moxy Show
Happily Ever After: Fairy Tales for Every Child
The Immortals
Panther

1996 *Martin*
Sgt. Bilko
Homicide: Life on the Street

1997 *Beverly Hills Ninja*

1998	*Lethal Weapon 4*
	Doctor Dolittle
	King of the Hill
1999	*Dogma*
2000	*Nurse Betty*
2001	*Down to Earth*
	Jay and Silent Bob Strike Back
	Osmosis Jones
	Pootie Tang
	Artificial Intelligence: AI
2002	*Bad Company*
2003	*Head of State*
2004	*Paparazzi*
2005	*Madagascar*
	The Longest Yard
2007	*I Think I Love My Wife*
	Bee Movie
2005–08	*Everybody Hates Chris*
2008	*Madagascar: Escape 2 Africa*

Albums

1991	*Born Suspect*
1997	*Roll with the New*
1999	*Bigger and Blacker*
2004	*Never Scared*
2007	*Cheese and Crackers: The Greatest Bits*

Books

Carr, David. "Hard at Work on New Year's Eve," *New York Times* (December 28, 2007): p. 1.

Townsend, Bob. "America's Funnyman Every Bit Family Man." *Atlanta Journal-Constitution* (March 18, 2007): p. L1.

Waldman, Alison J. "Everybody Can Watch 'Chris' Together." *Television Week* vol. 26, no. 44 (December 3, 2007): pp. 30–32.

Web Sites

http://chrisrock.com

This site is the Internet home base for the superstar comedian. Here you can check on tour dates, buy his record albums, and download wallpaper and photos of Rock. There are also links to the latest news and articles about him as well as classic video clips from Rock's movies, such as the satires *I'm Gonna Git You Sucka* and *CB4*. You can even learn about Rock's charity work with the Salvation Army of Greater New York. *Warning*: This site contains explicit content.

http://www.imdb.com

The Internet Movie Database collects information on all things related to movies. See what movies Chris Rock has made and which ones are in the making. The site also includes biographical information on the star and fun trivia to impress your friends. For example, did you know that in 1993 Paramount Pictures offered Rock the role of Lamont Sanford in a movie remake of the 1970s television show *Sanford and Son*?

http://www.pbs.org

Search for the 2008 program *African American Lives 2* and see scholar Henry Louis Gates and a host of black stars, including Rock, uncover their rich ancestry. During the series, Rock learned that his great-great grandfather, Julius Caesar Tingman, fought for the Union during the Civil War.

Publisher's note:

The Web sites mentioned in this book were active at the time of publication. The publisher is not responsible for Web sites that have changed their addresses or discontinued operation since the date of publication. The publisher will review and update the Web site addresses each time the book is reprinted.

Academy Awards—annual awards given by the Academy of Motion Picture Arts and Sciences, also known as the Oscars.

agents—somebody who officially represents someone else in business.

arrogant—feeling or showing self-importance and contempt or disregard for others.

black power—a movement formed by black people to achieve social equality and emphasize pride in their racial identity.

blaxploitation—depiction of black people in movies or other media in a way that appeals to popular and often inaccurate or negative notions of their experiences and qualities.

charitable—dispensing help to needy people.

discrimination—an act of bias or unfairness against people unlike oneself.

gigs—a show business term meaning performance or concert.

lemur—a primate with a long snout, large ears, and a long tail; native to Madagascar.

profane—irreverent and disrespectful.

sketch comedy—a brand of comedy in which actors play popular television and movie personalities in short scenes.

tirade—an angry outburst or lecture.

typecast—when an actor is placed in a similar role again and again.

UNICEF—a United Nations agency that works for the protection and survival of children around the world.

Chapter 1: The Big Time

page 6   "I agree not to curse . . ." Josh Wolk, "The Oscars Get Rock-ed." (January 31, 2005). *Entertainment Weekly* http:// www.ew.com/ew/article/0,,1021799,00.html

page 9   "They always write that . . ." Bill Zehme, "Chris Rock Isn't Laughing." *Rolling Stone* (April 3, 2008):, p. 50.

Chapter 2: The Brooklyn Boy Gets His Shot

page 12   "I figure that laughter . . . " *Rolling Stone*, "Chris Rock Hits his Hollywood Stride." (January 29, 2001). http://www.rollingstone.com/artists/chrisrock/articles/story/5920132/rolling_rock_chris_rock_hits_his_hollywood_stride.

page 15   "'Saturday Night Live' was the . . . " *Starpulse Entertainment News Blog*, "Chris Rock Sits Down with James Lipton." (March 9, 2007). http://www.starpulse.com/news/index.php/2007/03/09/chris_rock_sits_down_with_james_lipton_o_12.

page 15   "Sometimes I hate life . . . " Chris Rock, *Rock This* (New York: Hyperion, 1997), 9.

Chapter 3: The Bad with the Good

page 18   "I am African American . . ." *Time*, "Ten Questions" (March 26, 2007): pp. 4–6.

page 18   "You hear black people . . . " *Best of the Chris Rock Show 2*, HBO Home Video (1997).

page 20   "It's beyond my wildest . . ." "Chris Rock talks about his comedy, new wife and fame," *Jet* 92, no. 22 (October 20, 1997), p32.

page 25   "I'm from like . . ." *Friday Night with Jonathan Ross*, BBC-1 (January 11, 2008).

Chapter 4: Taking Control

page 27   "[Rock and Tucker] are attempting . . ." Justin Driver, "Mirth of a Nation." *New Republic* (June 11, 2001): pp. 29–33.

page 30   "Right now, where I am . . . " Larry King, *The Greatest Interviews*, Disc 3. DVD. (Warner Home Video., 2007).

page 33   "The rhythms are all over . . ." Lisa Schwarzbaum, "The Running Man: Chris Rock Demonstrates Leadership Ability in his Directing Debut," *Entertainment Weekly* 703 (April 4, 2003), p. 75.

page 35   "They're rich kids . . ." *Friday Night with Jonathan Ross*.

Chapter 5: Comedy Legend in the Making

page 37   "In this era . . . " Allison J. Waldman, "Everybody Can Watch 'Chris' Together," *Television Week* (December 3, 2007): pp. 30–32.

page 44   "Barack Obama . . . " Zehme, "Chris Rock Isn't Laughing," p. 46.

page 44   "In many ways . . ." David Hiltbrand, "Chris Rock's Campaign," *Philadelphia Inquirer* (February 28, 2008): pp. E1 and E3.

page 45   "The times compel him . . ." Bill Zehme, "Chris Rock Isn't Laughing." *Rolling Stone* (April 3, 2008):, p. 46.

Numbers in **bold italics** refer to captions.

David Robson is an award-winning writer and English professor. He is the recipient of a National Endowment for the Arts grant and two playwriting fellowships from the Delaware Division of the Arts. Aside from Chris Rock, his favorite all-time comedians include Richard Pryor and Steve Martin. Robson lives with his wife and daughter in Wilmington, Delaware.

PICTURE CREDITS

page

1: DreamWorks/FilmMagic

4: Abaca Press/KRT

7: New York Daily News/KRT

8: Orange County Register/KRT

10: London Features Int'l

13: Paramount Pictures/NMI

14: NBC/PRMS

16: DreamWorks/NMI

19: HBO/NMI

21: Orange County Register/KRT

23: Styleworks/PRMS

24: Warner Bros./NMI

26: HBO/NMI

29: Paramount Pictures/NMI

31: Touchstone Pictures/NMI

33: Abaca Press/KRT

34: DreamWorks/NMI

36: Annie Leibovitz/Gap Inc./PRMS

39: UPN/CW/NMI

40: Splash News

41: Fox Searchlight Pictures/NMI

43: infusny-1/INFGoff

47: Columbia Pictures/NMI

48: Bob Long/HFPA/PRMS

49: NBC/PRMS

51: Universal Pictures/NMI

52: 20th Century Fox/NMI

53: FPS/PRMS

55: Newswire/PRMS

Front cover: Annie Leibovitz/Gap Inc./PRMS